Above: Cirrostratus
Left: Stratocumulus
Below left: Altocumulus ("mackerel sky")
Below: Nimbostratus

Left: Cumulonimbus

U.S. Air Force Photo

Above: Altostratus over stratocumulus
Right: Stratus
Below: Cirrus ("mares' tails")

U.S. Weather Bureau

Below right: Cirrocumulus
Below: Cumulus

American Museum of Natural History

American Museum of Natural History

Florida State News Bureau

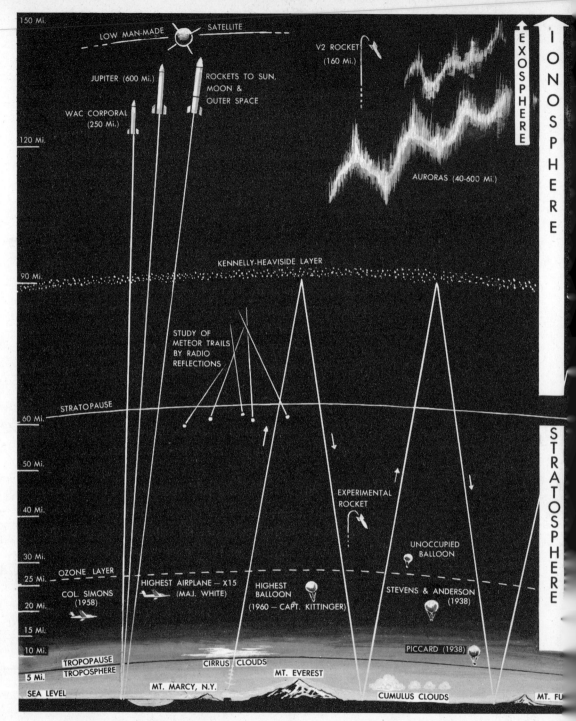

Cross-section of the shell of air that surrounds our planet. Scientists are generally agreed that there are four atmospheric layers — the troposphere, the stratosphere, the ionosphere, and the exosphere.

The FIRST BOOK of
AIR

A Basic Guide to the Earth's Atmosphere

by David C. Knight

Illustrated with Photographs and Drawings

FRANKLIN WATTS, INC.
575 Lexington Avenue, New York 22

Right: Capt. Joseph Kittinger parachuting from balloon at stratospheric level of 76,400

Library of Congress Catalog Card Number 61-6087

Author's and publisher's thanks to Ernest J. Christie, U.S. Weather Bureau, for his helpful suggestions concerning the manuscript of this book; and to those organizations, public and private, who generously supplied photographic materials. Line illustrations were drawn by Peter Costanza.

Printed in the United States of America
by Polygraphic Company of America

2   3   4   5

Operation "Skyhook." Ten-million-cubic-foot research balloon being launched from the U.S.S. *Valley Forge* off the Virgin Islands.

U.S. Navy

Contents

The Air Around Us

AIR is something that is all around us all the time. We live in a deep ocean of it, much as fish live in an ocean of water. We walk about in air. We fly through it. Awake and asleep, we breathe it from the moment we are born to the moment we die. Each of us uses up about 6000 gallons of it a day.

Air is spread throughout every part of our bodies. It is in the ground beneath our feet. Thousands of pounds of air constantly press down on us from above. And yet we can neither see, smell, nor taste air. Seldom are we ever aware of its tremendous weight.

How Do We Know That Air Is There?

Is AIR real? Does it take up space? If we can't see it, how do we know it is everywhere around us?

You can answer these questions by doing a few simple experiments.

Take an ordinary drinking straw and blow through it. Do you see anything coming out the other end? No, because air cannot be seen. But put the end of the straw under some water and blow through it as before. Although you still cannot see air, you can see air *bubbles* rise to the surface.

Go into the bathroom and fill the sink with water. Take a drinking glass, turn it upside down, and push it straight down into the water. Does the water go into the glass? No, because there is something *already* in the glass — air. Now jam some cotton into the bottom of the glass and repeat the experiment. Is the cotton still dry? Yes, because the air in the glass has stopped the water from getting in and wetting the cotton.

Try putting a number of different things under water; for example, a piece of wood or chalk, a dry sponge, a piece of cloth, a length of rope.

6

Note that some of these things send more air bubbles to the surface than others.

The next time you are with a group of friends, watch how each person *inhales* — takes air into his body. Watch their chests expand. You can even have a "chest expansion contest." Get a tape measure and measure whose expansion is the greatest. Try to see who can blow up the biggest balloon with just one breath of air.

By doing these simple experiments, you have already proved a number of things about air. You have proved 1. that air cannot be seen; 2. that air takes up room; 3. that spaces we think of as "empty" are really filled with air; 4. that some things contain more air than others; 5. that when air fills a space, it keeps other things out of that space; and, 6. that air is in our bodies.

Most important of all, you have proved that air is a real substance and that it is everywhere about us.

What If There Were No Air?

WITHOUT air we could not make a fire or cook our meals. Without air most sounds would not reach us. Without air plants could not grow. Without air there would be no water, and the earth's surface would be as oceanless as the moon's. Without air to breathe, we could not live, nor could any of the earthly creatures we know.

The protective blanket of air that surrounds our earth is much like the glass roof that covers a greenhouse. It lessens the extremes of heat and cold between night and day, summer and winter. Air can do this because it traps the heat of the sun's rays so that it escapes more slowly into space, at the same time that it warms the earth. The moon, which has no blanket of air about it, suffers greatly from severe temperature changes. During the great heat of the lunar day, temperatures can reach

7

The Willamette Meteorite standing in the first-floor corridor at the Hayden Planetarium in New York City. It was found near Oregon City, Oregon, in 1902, and weighs 15½ tons.

the boiling point of water and at night they can drop as low as 200° below zero Fahrenheit.

The air above the earth also shelters man from a steady rain of meteors that would otherwise make his life a nightmare. *Meteors,* sometimes called "shooting stars," are pieces of stony or metallic rock in outer space. Most of them are as small as grains of sand; others are as huge as giant boulders. Billions and billions of them are widely scattered throughout our solar systems. Scientists have estimated that more than a hundred billion meteors strike the earth's blanket of air every twenty-four hours! Luckily, all but a tiny fraction of them are reduced to gas and dust through friction when they hit the air above us. Those that do get through and land on the earth are called *meteorites.*

If there were no air, there would be no weather. *Weather* is the word we use in talking about how hot or cold or wet or dry the air is; whether it is calm or stormy, clear or cloudy. It is because of the changes in the air around and above us that we have various kinds of weather. If there were no air, there could be no falling rain, no changing winds, no shifting clouds. Nor would there be the blue of the daytime sky nor any rainbows, for without air, the sky would be forever black.

8

Does Air Move?

ON A breezy day, watch some clouds or the smoke coming from a chimney. Are they moving all by themselves? No; it is the air disturbance we call wind that carries the smoke and the clouds along. *Wind* is air that is moving. Wind is also what makes a flag wave and causes the branches of trees to sway.

When the wind is blowing, toss some light object like a stick up in the air. Does it fall straight back down again? No — the wind carries it along a little way before it falls. Find or make a paper pin wheel and hold it up. The wind will make it spin around.

Now take the pin wheel inside where there is no wind. You can make it spin just the same by making a fan and fanning the pin wheel very hard. Put some small pieces of paper on a table and see how easily you can blow them off by fanning them.

By doing these simple experiments you have learned three things. 1. Moving air — *wind* — carries things along with it. 2. Moving air pushes against things. 3. We can make our own "wind" by making air move.

What Is Air Made Of?

WE REALLY live *on* one gigantic sphere, and *inside* another, much larger one! The first sphere is the solid earth beneath our feet. The second is the vast layer of air that completely surrounds the earth.

This great blanket of air covers every bit of the earth's surface. It reaches upward to a height of about 700 miles; after that, it gradually thins out into space. This outer shell of air that surrounds our planet is called the *atmosphere,* meaning a "sphere of vapor."

Air is what the atmosphere is made of. It is a mixture of colorless, invisible gases. The gas called *nitrogen* makes up about four-fifths of

9

U.S. Navy Photo

the atmosphere; the gas called *oxygen* makes up about one-fifth.

When you bake a cake or make some fudge, you follow a recipe. If you were to "make" a certain quantity of what is known as *pure dry air,* you would follow a recipe, too. Let's say you wanted to make a "loaf" of pure dry air. The ingredients you would need would be these: 78 parts of nitrogen; 21 parts of oxygen; 9/10 of a part of argon; 3/100 of a part of carbon dioxide; and very much smaller fractional parts of the gases krypton, neon, xenon, hydrogen, helium, and ozone.

The trouble is, however, that pure dry air does not occur in nature. First of all, there are always varying quantities of water vapor in the air. Second, there are always impurities in the air such as dust particles.

The Air's Ingredients and What They Do

ALTHOUGH air seems to be "all one thing," we have seen that it is really a mixture of separate ingredients. Most of these remain separate rather than form chemical compounds. In part, this is because most of them are *elements*. An *element* is a substance that cannot be separated by ordinary chemical means into different substances. While it is true that there are chemical compounds in the air, such as carbon dioxide and water vapor, the main substances that make up air do not vary greatly in their mixture over the earth's surface.

Let us look at these gases and see what part each plays in our atmosphere.

Nitrogen makes up the largest part of the air. It thins out the other,

10

heavier main element of air — oxygen — much as water does lemon juice in lemonade. Nitrogen is essential for plant growth; therefore, it is valuable to us as plant (vegetable and fruit) eaters.

Oxygen makes up the next largest part of the air. It is the substance that all living things must have to convert food into vital energy. Also, without oxygen *combustion*, or burning, could not take place.

Carbon dioxide is one of the chemical compounds of the air, and is made up of one part carbon and two parts oxygen. Carbon dioxide is the gaseous waste product we exhale in the breathing process. But it is also the main substance that plants use for food. Carbon dioxide is also valuable in holding in the earth's heat.

Neon, argon, xenon, and *krypton* are called *inert* gases because they do not combine with other elements. Although they are of little known importance in the air, neon is used in advertising signs, and argon in electric light bulbs.

Helium and *hydrogen* are very scarce in air, except at great heights. Being the lightest of all gases, they are used inside balloons and other lighter-than-air craft for lifting purposes.

Ozone is a very active, pure, "supercharged" form of oxygen. It is the only gas in the air that has an odor.

Water vapor is present in the air in great quantities as a gas. It gets into the air by evaporating from oceans, lakes, swamps, and rivers. Like other gases, it is colorless and invisible. Although we rarely see this water, it is there just the same, like a big invisible ocean overhead. Besides carbon dioxide, water vapor is the other chemical compound in the air in large quantities and is composed of two parts hydrogen and one part oxygen.

Water vapor is one of the most important gases in the air because when it condenses (changes back to a liquid), it forms clouds, which in turn produce the rainfall necessary to life. The amount of water vapor in the air varies with the climate. On a hot summer day, the air in an

11

average room could contain as much as three pounds of water vapor, or about a quart and a half in liquid form.

Dust is the general term for all the tiny impurities that are almost always present in the air. Dust, of course, is not a gas. It can consist of particles blown up from the soil or volcanoes; from burning fuel or forest fires; from meteors; from plants as pollen; from bacteria; or from salt particles whipped into the air by ocean sprays.

Dust particles are so small that most of them are invisible unless placed under a microscope. Their number in any given space varies from one place to another. Above mountains or over oceans there may be only a few thousand particles in a cubic centimeter. But over smoky cities, there may be as many as *5 million or more* in a cubic centimeter!

Dust is a very necessary part of our atmosphere. These tiny dust particles act as centers about which moisture collects. Without dust to cling to, water vapor could not condense out of the air in droplets. Hence, clouds would never form to release their moisture earthward as snow or rain. Heavy dews would then be the only way the earth could be watered because moisture, which needs a surface on which to condense, could only do so on foliage or the ground. Indeed, life would be quite different from the way we now know it if there were no dust in the air.

These, then, are the ingredients that make up air. But what, you may be wondering, keeps all this air in place around the earth? Why does it not simply float away into space? The answer is, it cannot. The earth holds all of these gases to it by the powerful pull of gravity.

How High Does the Atmosphere Go?

HIGH-FLYING jet pilots and even mountain climbers know that the air grows thinner the higher up they go. As little as two miles above the

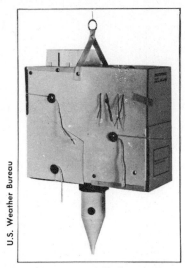

U.S. Weather Bureau

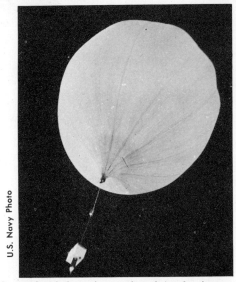

U.S. Navy Photo

Right: a navy research balloon carrying a radiosonde aloft at the south pole. Left: closeup of a radiosonde; it carries a thermometer, barometer, hygrometer, and a radio transmitter.

earth, human beings find it difficult to breathe. Pilots flying much above 10,000 feet must carry an oxygen supply with them in order to breathe. Just how high does our atmosphere go?

Man himself has recently flown to an altitude of 131,000 feet in a rocket-powered research aircraft, but his actual investigation of the atmosphere has gone far beyond this height. By means of radio equipment (called *radiosondes*) in balloons, radar, rockets, sound explosions, and artificial satellites, information has been transmitted back from altitudes many times higher than man himself has flown. As new satellites are launched man will increase his knowledge of the atmosphere and of outer space.

By studying meteor trails — as well as other methods — scientists believe that the atmosphere extends upward for 700 miles or more. They also tell us that the atmosphere exists *in layers*. Each of these layers can be distinguished from the others, even though one tends to merge into another. Also, no layer stays in one place all the time, or even stays the same size. In fact, each can change hourly in thickness.

13

The bottom layer of air is the one we live in. It is called the *troposphere*. The names comes from the Greek word *tropos,* meaning "turn," since the air in this layer is always turning and rushing about. Because winds here can move up and down and back and forth, the troposphere is the layer of our familiar weather changes. About 80 per cent of the air by weight is packed into the troposphere.

The up and down winds of the troposphere are called *currents. Up currents* can carry gliders and insects high into the troposphere. Spiders, for example, have been captured as high as five miles up.

The troposphere is generally about five miles high at the north and south pole, and about ten miles high at the equator. The higher up you go in the troposphere, the colder it gets. The temperature drops about 1° Fahrenheit with every 300 feet of increasing altitude.

The dividing limit marking the top of the troposphere is called the *tropopause*. At this altitude the temperature does not fall any longer. In general, the warmer the climate at sea level, the higher the tropopause will be.

Wrapped around the tropopause is the next highest layer called the *stratosphere,* from the Latin word *stratum* meaning "layer" or "covering." This layer extends about 50 miles above the tropopause and about 60 miles above the earth. The stratosphere is the region of strong, steady winds that generally move parallel to the earth's surface. There is practically no water vapor or dust in the stratosphere and the skies are nearly always clear. These conditions make the stratosphere a good region for aircraft to fly in; in fact, planes designed to fly there are sometimes called "stratocruisers" or "stratoliners." Passengers of such aircraft, however, must always be protected against the lack of oxygen, the low pressure due to less air, and the extreme cold.

At the tropopause, where the stratosphere begins, the temperature is about 67° Fahrenheit below zero. But the higher you go above this point into the stratosphere, the warmer the temperature becomes, until an altitude of about 28 miles is reached. The temperature at this level reaches 90° Fahrenheit above zero or higher. Then the temperature begins to drop again to well below freezing. The outer limit of the stratosphere, about 60 miles above the earth's surface, is called the *stratopause*.

In the stratosphere, about 25 miles above the earth, is the *ozone layer*. Ozone soaks up the powerful ultraviolet rays from the sun. If the ozone layer were not there, these powerful rays would get through and literally sunburn us to death. Of course, some of this ultraviolet light does get through — but just enough to change certain substances into Vitamin D, which is necessary for health. Amazingly enough, this ozone layer is so thin that if it were under the same great pressure as the air at the earth's surface, it would be pressed into a shell only one-tenth of an inch thick!

Above the stratosphere is the *ionosphere*. It is so called because it contains vast numbers of *ions,* or electrified air particles. Here the air is very thin. The high electrification is caused for the most part by the

A 72-ton Boeing Stratocruiser.

Boeing Airplane Co.

sun's powerful ultraviolet rays. The ionosphere extends from the strato-pause to a height of about 300 miles above the surface of the earth. Scientists tell us that here the temperature rises steadily with increasing altitude and that they believe readings of nearly as high as 4000° Fahr-enheit above zero are possible! Space ships that hope to reach the moon or the neighboring planets will not only have to overcome these intense temperatures, but also the many electrical dangers of the ionosphere.

In the ionosphere there are certain regions where more electrified air particles collect than in others. Perhaps the best known of these highly electrified layers is the Kennelly-Heaviside Layer. It, and other layers at other levels, are of great value because they reflect radio waves back to earth. If it were not for such electrical "mirrors," radio messages could not be sent such great distances. The waves bounce back and forth, again and again — even around the earth — making it possible for us to hear programs from distant cities.

Sometimes these electrified ions produce beautiful color effects known as *auroras*. They are generally caused by *sunspots*, powerful disturb-ances on the sun, which charge the upper air with electricity. The *aurora*

Left: photo of *aurora borealis*, or "northern lights"; right: an old print of a double auroral arc that occurred in 1902.

American Museum of Natural

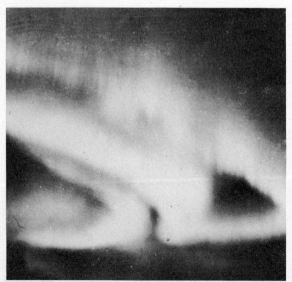

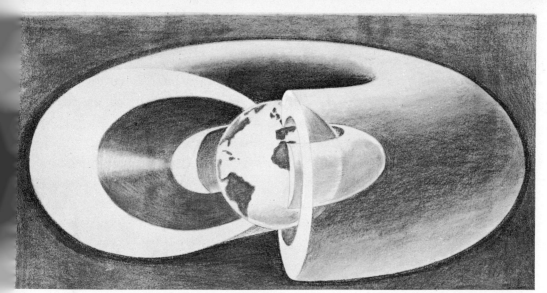

The Van Allen Radiation Belts, showing doughnut-within-a-doughnut structure.

borealis, which occurs in the northern regions, is sometimes called the "northern lights." The *aurora australis,* in the southern hemisphere, is known as the "southern lights."

Above the ionosphere is the layer known as the *exosphere* about which very little is known. In the exosphere what little air is left in the atmosphere gradually merges with the blackness of interplanetary space.

What Are the Van Allen Radiation Belts?

WHEN America's first Explorer satellites were put into orbit about the earth in 1958, they carried instruments that sent back valuable information to scientists on earth. One of these scientists, Dr. James A. Van Allen, began to study this information closely. He found out that there were two bands of deadly radiation surrounding the earth high above the exosphere.

Named after Dr. Van Allen, the Van Allen belts are made up of highly-charged electrified particles trapped in the earth's magnetic field. They are both in the shape of huge doughnuts. One is inside the other. The inner belt seems to be made up of radioactive particles coming from the earth. The strongest part of this inner belt is about 2000 miles from

17

the earth. It is believed that the outer Van Allen belt's particles originate on the sun. The strongest part of the outer belt is about 10,000 miles above the earth's equator.

Since space ships of the future will have to pass through these dangerous Van Allen radiation belts, scientists will have to learn much more about them.

Air Has Weight

NORMALLY we are not aware that air has weight and that the atmosphere pushes with tremendous force on our bodies all the time. Right this minute this "invisible giant" is pressing with a force of many tons on your body. The reason you don't feel this pressure is that the air inside your body is pushing back with the same force. There are probably several hundred pounds of air in the room you are sitting in right now.

The reason why air has such tremendous weight near the earth's surface is because the gas molecules that make it up can be *compressed* — squeezed together — when pressure is put on them. When pressure is taken off them, they can expand.

Air can even compress itself. Think back to the layers of the atmosphere you have just read about. Each of those layers presses down on the ones below it, squeezing the air more and more nearer the earth's surface. This means that there is more air packed into a given space close to the earth than there is in the same amount of space in the outer layers of the atmosphere. Scientists would say that the air is *denser* the nearer it is to the earth — that is, its particles, called molecules, are closer together, and more of them are crammed into a given space.

You can imagine this very easily. Think of the layers of the atmosphere as a high stack of pancakes. Although the pancakes are made of

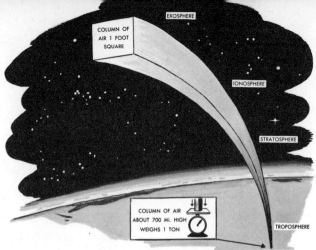

COLUMN OF
AIR 1 FOOT
SQUARE

EXOSPHERE

IONOSPHERE

STRATOSPHERE

COLUMN OF AIR
ABOUT 700 Mi. HIGH
WEIGHS 1 TON

TROPOSPHERE

the same thing, those on the bottom are squeezed flat, while the ones nearest the top are still thick and fluffy.

The bottommost "pancake" — our troposphere — is where there is the most air, and where air is the heaviest. Half the total weight of all the air in the atmosphere lies within 3½ miles of the surface of the earth, and 99 per cent lies below the 20-mile limit.

At sea level a cubic foot of air weighs a little more than 1.2 ounces. While this does not seem like very much, the weight of more and more air can mount up very quickly. Scientists have figured out that the total weight of all the air in our atmosphere weighs something like 5,810 million *million* tons!

If you could cut out a column of air one foot square extending right up to the top of the atmosphere, that column would be pushing with a force of just about one ton on a square foot of the earth's surface. This works out to mean that the weight of air at sea level is pressing down with a force of about 15 pounds on every square inch of the earth's surface.

You can prove that air has weight by actually weighing some. Get a basketball or football and weigh it on a scale while it is inflated. Then deflate the ball and weigh it again. The difference between the two weights will be the weight of the air the ball contained.

You can also demonstrate the great crushing power that air pressure

has right in your school laboratory. Get an empty one-gallon oil can and remove the air from it. (When all, or nearly all, of the air is removed from such a container, the empty space is called a *vacuum*.) As more and more of a vacuum is reached, the can will slowly collapse due to the air pushing in on it from the outside in all directions. The same thing could happen to a big building if it were airtight, not strongly built, and if all the air were removed from inside it.

Air Pressure and How It Is Measured

IN THE seventeenth century, Otto von Guericke, the German Mayor of Magdeburg, did some of the first experiments with air pressure. Perhaps his most famous one was done with two hollow bronze bowls, called *hemispheres*.

Von Guericke took a pair of these hemispheres, fitted them tightly together, and removed the air from inside them. Before the German emperor and his court, he showed that two teams of horses pulling in opposite directions could not pull the hemispheres apart. The air pressure outside them kept them tightly together. Yet when von Guericke

let the air back into the closed hemispheres they could be separated with the slightest touch.

The first man to successfully measure air pressure was Evangelista Torricelli (pronounced tor-re-*chel*-le) in 1643. Torricelli was a pupil of the Italian scientist, Galileo. For years Galileo had wondered why an ordinary pump could not raise water in a pipe higher than 34 feet. Galileo died before he could find out, leaving the problem to his pupil.

Torricelli figured out that it was the weight of the air on the water inside the pump that pushed the water up. The limit that the air could do this was 34 feet and no more.

Torricelli decided to see how the pressure of the atmosphere acted on other liquids, since working with a 34-foot tube of water was clumsy. Using mercury in a tube, Torricelli made a famous experiment upon which the principle of the barometer is based. A *barometer* is an instrument used to measure air pressure. Torricelli made the first effective one in 1643.

You can do the same experiment that Torricelli did, and at the same time make a homemade mercury barometer. Take a heavy glass tube a little more than 30 inches long, closed at one end. Fill up the tube completely with mercury. Seal the tube tight at the open end by pressing your finger over it. At the same time turn the tube upside down and put it in a dish of mercury. With the open end under the mercury, remove your finger.

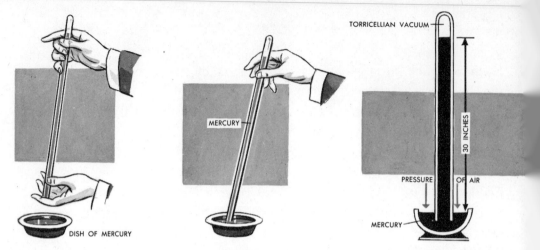

TORRICELLIAN VACUUM

30 INCHES

PRESSURE OF AIR

MERCURY

MERCURY

DISH OF MERCURY

Torricelli's experiment.

Now watch the mercury in the tube. It will drop, but not very far. The empty space in the top of the tube is not filled with air, but a vacuum. A vacuum made this way is still called a *Torricellian vacuum*.

Next get a yardstick and measure the column of mercury in the tube. You will find — just as Torricelli did — that at sea level it stands just about 30 inches high. The mercury is held at that height in the tube by air pressure pushing down on the mercury in the dish. Thus Torricelli knew that normal air pressure at sea level was 30 inches.

When such a tube is fitted out with a mercury well and a measuring scale, either in inches or centimeters, it becomes the same *mercury barometer* that is generally in use today. The changes in daily atmospheric pressure cause corresponding changes in the readings on the scale. When air pressure increases, the mercury rises; when it lessens, the mercury falls. Mercury barometers are very accurate and are used by weather bureaus today.

Mercury barometers, however, are not easy to carry about, so a smaller *aneroid barometer* is often used instead. *Aneroid* means "without liquid;" aneroid barometers have no liquid inside them. If you have a barometer at home, it is probably the aneroid kind.

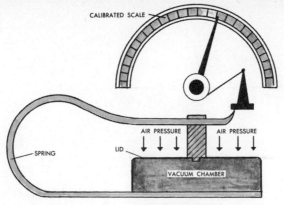

Diagram of an aneroid barometer.

The diagram above shows how simply the aneroid barometer works. If the air is taken out of a small, flat box, the lid of the box will be pushed down by the pressure of the air. The greater the pressure, the farther down the sensitive lid will be pushed. If the pressure lessens, the lid springs back up. On top of the lid are attached a series of springs and levers and, finally, a pointer that moves along a scale marked off in inches. This scale is "calibrated" so that it reads the same as that of the mercury barometer. Thus, any change in the pressure of the air on the lid of the box will show up as a reading on the scale.

How Air Pressure Changes at Different Altitudes

In 1648, the French scientist, Blaise Pascal, had one of Torricelli's mercury barometers carried up the famous Puy-de-Dôme Mountain in France. Pascal suspected that the great pressure of the air would be less at the top of a mountain than at sea level. The only way to find out was to put some of the atmosphere *below* the barometer by carrying it to the top of the nearly 5000-foot-high Puy-de-Dôme.

Pascal found out that the higher the barometer was brought up the mountain, the lower the mercury dropped in the tube. At the very top of the Puy-de-Dôme, the column of mercury stood only 27 inches high, compared with 30 inches at sea level. This proved that the pressure of

Taylor Instrument Companies

Above: various models of aneroid barometers, used to predict the weather. Below: two extra-sensitive recording barometers (barographs); delicate instruments like these give continuous written records that make possible accurate weather forecasts.

air was less at higher altitudes. The reason of course was that there was much less air pressing down.

A barometer will fall to about 15 inches at an altitude of 18,000 feet; twenty miles above the earth it will only register about half an inch. Although there is still air at an altitude of 50 miles, its pressure is so slight that it probably will not show on any instrument.

In general, a barometer will show a drop of just about one inch for each 900 feet of altitude in the first few thousand feet of the atmosphere. For example, if an aneroid barometer reads 30 inches at sea level, it will read 29 inches at a height of 900 feet. If the face dial of an aneroid barometer is marked off in feet instead of inches it is called an *altimeter*. An altimeter records an airplane's altitude above sea level.

From day to day throughout the world, the pressure of the air changes. These changes are due to the temperature and the amount of water vapor in the air. While those changes are often small, they are important because they act as signposts for predicting what the weather will be. A "falling" barometer usually tells that storm clouds, rain, or snow are coming. A "rising" barometer usually predicts the coming of fair weather.

Weather bureaus use an instrument called a *barograph* to record changes in air pressure. It is really an aneroid barometer with a pen for an indicator instead of a pointer. The barograph records air pressure automatically. A scale sheet is attached to a rotating cylinder and on it the pen records the daily changes in air pressure.

How Man Puts Air to Work

BEFORE the time of Galileo, it was believed that air could not possibly be used to do work because it weighed less than nothing! Today of

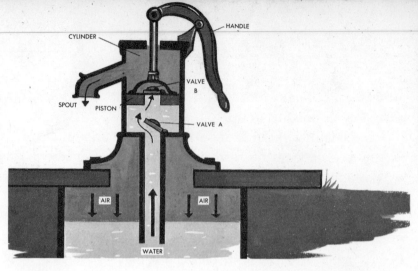

How a simple lift pump works. When piston moves up on upstroke, valve A opens and pressure of outside air forces water up into cylinder. When piston moves down on downstroke, valve B opens and valve A shuts. Water is forced out through spout on second upstroke.

course, we know that air has weight and that its pressure is tremendous. That pressure — and the way molecules of air behave generally — is an important source of power for all mankind.

The common pump (above), used for lifting water, has been used for centuries by man. But the ordinary air pressure that works a pump is not powerful enough to operate modern tools such as rock drills and air hammers.

To run these tools, a much greater source of power is needed. Such powerful devices can be made to work for man by *compressing*, or squeezing, air so that its weight and energy is increased.

What happens when air is compressed?

In the seventeenth century, an English chemist, Robert Boyle, noticed how *elastic* air was. Boyle called it "the spring of the air." He first noticed how air could be compressed by a famous experiment. Pouring mercury into a U-shaped tube closed at one end, he found that the air trapped in the closed end had indeed become "squeezed."

Today, we know that air molecules are darting and bouncing about all the time. They move at speeds of over 200 miles an hour and bump into each other *many millions of times* a second! Robert Boyle did not know this, but he did discover a famous law that says how these molecules behave when they are placed in a container.

If air is enclosed in a bottle, the molecules of air strike the inside of

26

the bottle all the time with a push of ordinary air pressure — about 15 pounds on a square inch of the bottle. Boyle's Law says that if the same amount of air were forced into a bottle half that size, the air pressure of the molecules is doubled. If that same air were forced into a bottle one-tenth the size of the original one, there would be *ten times* as much pressure!

This is why compressed air can supply such great power for modern tools. *Air compressors,* which work much like the simple pump described above, squeeze ordinary air into steel tanks or containers under heavy pressure.

These tanks of compressed air stand ready to serve man everywhere. In every gasoline station there is one available to pump up a car's tires, to elevate a car lift, and to perform many other services. Even the bicycle pump you use to pump up your bike's tires is a simple kind of air compressor.

Compressed air works for us in many other ways too. It can be used

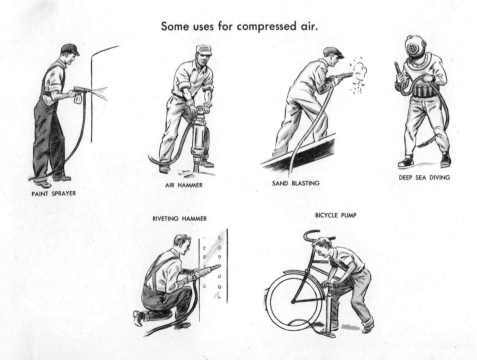

Some uses for compressed air.

PAINT SPRAYER   AIR HAMMER   SAND BLASTING   DEEP SEA DIVING

RIVETING HAMMER   BICYCLE PUMP

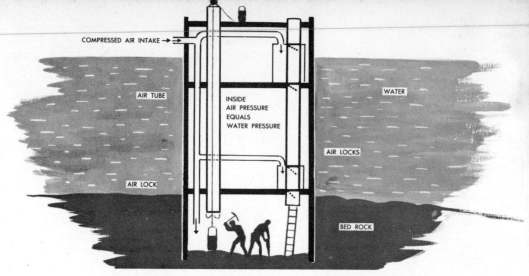

COMPRESSED AIR INTAKE →

AIR TUBE

INSIDE
AIR PRESSURE
EQUALS
WATER PRESSURE

WATER

AIR LOCKS

AIR LOCK

BED ROCK

A caisson, used for underwater work.

to spray paint and insecticides. It operates the powerful "air brakes" on trucks and trains. "Air hammers," connected directly to powerful air compressor pumps, are used to rip up street pavements. Compressed air drills can cut through solid rock, and rivet heavy steel beams together.

Compressed air is valuable, too, for keeping water and mud out of *caissons* — underwater chambers in which men must work while building underwater foundations or erecting piers in water. The compressed air inside the working area keeps the air pressure just equal to the pressure of the water outside. Otherwise the caisson would collapse on the workmen inside.

When the pressure of the air is *reduced* in certain places, thus mak-

Left: principle of the vacuum cleaner. Right: a modern vacuum cleaner.

TO DUST BAG

REDUCED AIR PRESSURE

The Hoover Co.

A modern pavement breaker in action. The compressed air is piped from the compressed air tank through a hose to the breaker. The man merely guides the breaker; the compressed air supplies the energy that does the work.

ing a *partial vacuum,* it can also do work for man. This is how the *vacuum* cleaner got its name. A fan in the cleaner reduces the air pressure just above the rug, allowing the normal air pressure beneath the rug to push the dirt up past the fan and into a dust bag.

The same thing happens when you breathe. When you inhale a breath of air, the space around your lungs is increased and the air pressure inside your body is reduced. The greater pressure of the air outside your body then pushes the air into your lungs.

Why We Must Have Air to Breathe

ALL living creatures, from man to the smallest animal called an amoeba, must breathe in order to live. The reason for breathing is to get oxygen. Some tiny animals, such as earthworms, get their oxygen by "breathing" it in through their skin. But man gets his oxygen from the air that he takes through his nostrils or his mouth. It then enters his lungs by means of a tube called the *windpipe.*

Breathing, or *respiration,* is something that every living creature goes through in the same way. Oxygen is forced into the system and a waste

29

product, carbon dioxide, is driven out. In man, the carbon dioxide leaves by the same channel as the air originally went in — the windpipe. However, man does his real breathing *inside* his body. That is where the all-important oxygen comes in. What happens to it inside the human body?

When air is drawn into the lungs, the red cells of the blood stream absorb the oxygen from it. The blood stream then carries these red cells throughout the whole body. The red cells give up their oxygen to the cells of other tissues in the body such as muscles and glands, which need it to manufacture food. Then the red cells return to the lungs for more oxygen. Thus the process of breathing goes on and on. If that process stops, life stops, too.

The oxygen in our bodies combines with the food we eat, as well as tissues, in a process called *oxidation*. Oxidation is what produces the heat and energy our bodies require. Usually our normal body temperature is about 98° Fahrenheit.

When we exercise our bodies in any way, we must breathe more quickly. This is because we need more oxygen so that our bodily oxidation rate can go on faster. Also, more of the waste product, carbon dioxide, has to be gotten rid of. Just sitting in a chair and reading this book, you would only need to take about eighteen breaths a minute. Young people usually breathe faster than older people because they are more active and oxidation goes on at a faster rate in their bodies.

Fish, too, must have oxygen to live, even though they live underwater. This means that there must be air present in water, just as there is water in air. You can prove that there is air dissolved in water by drawing a glass of water from a tap and letting it stand for a little while. Soon bubbles of air will form and rise to the surface of the glass.

Fish get their oxygen from the air dissolved in water. They take water through gills, or flaps, alongside their throats. Watch any fish in an aquarium. The fish is not "drinking" the water, he is breathing it.

30

How Nature Balances Air — The Oxygen-Carbon Dioxide Life Cycle

FOR OUR "loaf" of air on page 10, we needed 21 parts of oxygen and 3/100 of a part of carbon dioxide. These amounts never seem to change much in the air. Why, you might ask, is this so, since so much oxygen is being used up all the time? The breathing of men and animals consumes vast quantities of oxygen every minute. So does the burning of industrial fuels. And, the end-product of all these processes is always carbon dioxide.

Why then shouldn't the supply of oxygen in the air get less and less, and the carbon dioxide more and more?

Because nature always maintains a balance called the *oxygen-carbon dioxide life cycle*. The carbon dioxide that all living creatures give off in the breathing process is taken in — together with water — by green plants to manufacture foods, such as starch and sugar. But a gas is also produced — *oxygen*.

If plant life did not give back this oxygen to the surrounding air, animal life could not live for very long. Scientists have estimated that if the amount of carbon dioxide were increased to as little as 5 per cent of the air, both men and animals would die.

The process by which green plants take in carbon dioxide and water from the air to manufacture starch, sugar, and oxygen is called *photosynthesis*. This term comes from *photo,* meaning "light," and *synthesis,* "a putting together" — a "putting together with light."

Photosynthesis in plants can only take place in sunlight. It is the sun's energy that causes the carbon dioxide and water to combine to form the carbohydrates and the oxygen. For photosynthesis to work in plant life, two things must always be present: 1. sunlight; photosynthesis

31

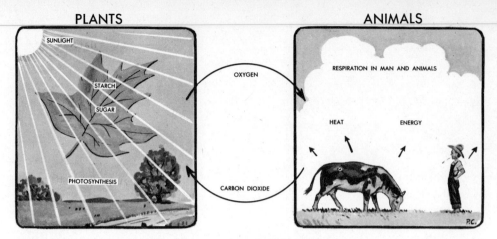

The oxygen-carbon dioxide life cycle.

cannot take place at night, and 2. the green pigment in plants called *chlorophyll;* no photosynthesis can occur without it.

Thus plant and animal life both help maintain the precious oxygen-carbon dioxide life cycle. What animals give up to the air through *respiration,* or breathing, plants must have for *photosynthesis.* And what plants in turn give up to the air through *photosynthesis,* animals must have for *respiration.*

How Water Vapor Gets Into the Air

AS WE KNOW, water vapor is present in large quantities in the atmosphere. Almost all of that water vapor lies in the troposphere. In the stratosphere, there is almost no water vapor at all.

How does all this water vapor get into the troposphere? Some of it is whipped up from oceans and lakes by strong winds, but most of it gets into the atmosphere by evaporation. *Evaporation* is the process by which liquid water is changed into its invisible gaseous state — water vapor.

Evaporation is a cooling process that allows molecules on any water surface to escape into the surrounding air. These molecules are always bouncing about, but the more they are heated the higher they bounce, and the easier they can escape into the air as water vapor. That is why

32

you feel cool after swimming. The heat from your body is being used to evaporate the water that is clinging to you.

The speed at which evaporation goes on depends on the size of the water surface and the condition of the surrounding air. The larger the surface, the faster the evaporation. Clothes on a line, for example, dry faster if they are spread out than if they are bunched up. A large lake will evaporate away more water than a small pond. And the warmer, drier, and windier it is, the speedier evaporation will be.

Water escapes into the troposphere as vapor at any place on the earth's surface where water exists. Even icy surfaces such as glaciers evaporate, though much more slowly than water in liquid form. Most water vapor enters the atmosphere by evaporating from lakes, oceans, rivers, and marshes. A much smaller amount gets into the air from moist earth, plants, and the breathing of men and animals.

How Much Water Vapor Can the Air Hold?

THE AMOUNT of water vapor in the air changes all the time. The amount in any one place depends almost entirely on the temperature of that place.

On a warm day, there is much more evaporation from lakes, oceans, streams, and other bodies of water. In general, the warmer the air is, the more water vapor it can hold. If there is a drop in the temperature and the air becomes colder, a part of the water vapor *condenses* (changes back to a liquid again) as rain, frost, or dew.

Just so much water vapor can evaporate into a given amount of air at any given temperature. At 30° Fahrenheit, a cubic foot of air can contain two weight-units of water vapor called *grains*. (About 400 grains make an ounce.) If the temperature goes up to 80° Fahrenheit, it can hold about eleven grains of water vapor. Such a cubic foot of water is then said to have reached a point called *capacity*. Capacity means the largest amount of water vapor a unit of air can hold at a certain temperature.

The higher the temperature goes, the higher capacity can be. When air is at capacity it is also said to be *saturated*, meaning "filled up." Water vapor is invisible until the space where it is becomes saturated; then it can be seen as droplets on the surface of things, or as fog.

Absolute and Relative Humidity

Humidity is the general word we use when we talk about the moisture in, or the dampness of, air. There are two kinds of humidity.

Absolute humidity means the actual amount of water vapor that a unit of air can hold at a given temperature. It is really another way of saying capacity.

Relative humidity is the term we hear most often in weather reports. It compares the amount of water vapor that is in the air with the greatest amount it *could* hold (capacity). Relative humidity is expressed in per cent.

For human beings to be comfortable, the relative humidity should be somewhere around 50 per cent, although the actual figure would vary with changing atmospheric conditions. If the relative humidity were 100 per cent, the air would be saturated, or at capacity.

"It isn't the heat, it's the humidity."

WE OFTEN hear people say this on uncomfortably hot summer days. What the statement really means is that the relative humidity has risen to the point where the air around us is much more saturated with water vapor than usual; the atmosphere just contains too much of it for comfort. Why?

Our bodies give off excess heat all the time in the form of moisture through the skin: we perspire or "sweat." Although our bodies continue to perspire when the air has too much water vapor in it (particularly when the temperature is high), there is no way our bodies can evaporate that moisture away. The outside air, already heavily laden with moisture, cannot absorb any more. Therefore we remain damp, and complain of feeling "sticky"and "muggy."

There are several instruments that measure relative humidity. One is a *hair hygrometer* (*hygro* means "moisture"). Human hair lengthens in moist air and shortens in dry air. A bundle of it is used in the hygrometer, its changes in length showing the relative humidity by means of a pointer on a scale.

The *hygrograph,* which is similar to the barograph, is an automatic hygrometer that keeps a continuous record of relative humidity.

Three forms of the hygrometer. Left: a wet-and-dry-bulb thermometer type with revolving table to show relative humidity. Lower right: a psychrometer type that is whirled with a chain. Upper right: a hair hygrograph that records relative humidity on a 7-day chart.

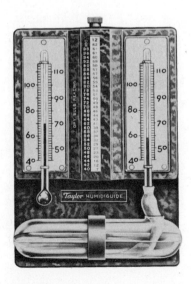

Taylor Instrument Companies

Ventilation

IF HUMAN BEINGS did not constantly have fresh air to breathe in theaters, classrooms, offices, mines, and other enclosed places, they would soon get sick. That is why such places must be kept supplied with fresh air by *ventilation* all the time.

Ventilation means to circulate air through closed spaces so as to get rid of the stale air and replace it with new. This new air also removes excess heat and brings with it fresh oxygen, which human beings need to live and work better. If a room is "stuffy" or "close" it means that the ventilation is poor and there is not enough fresh air to breathe. That is why you are apt to get a headache in a very crowded room; it has become filled with odors, smoke, and stale air.

In the average home a person needs from 15 to 20 cubic feet of fresh air *per minute* to be completely comfortable and to be able to work efficiently. (This does not mean a person *breathes* this much of course.) In larger places such as auditoriums, schools, theaters, and factories, people may need as many as 30 cubic feet.

There are two kinds of ventilation — *natural* and *mechanical*. If you are sitting in a closed room now, go over to the door and windows and feel around the cracks with your hand. Did you feel a light current of air seeping in? That is one kind of natural ventilation called *leakage*.

In an average home, leakage can provide adequate ventilation. Natural ventilation is also provided through open windows and doors. Factories and office buildings take advantage of ordinary drafts of rising warm air; this is allowed to escape through roof openings while newer air comes in at floor levels through windows or separately constructed openings.

Mechanical ventilation provides fresh air to large office buildings, theaters, and other places where large numbers of people gather. Since

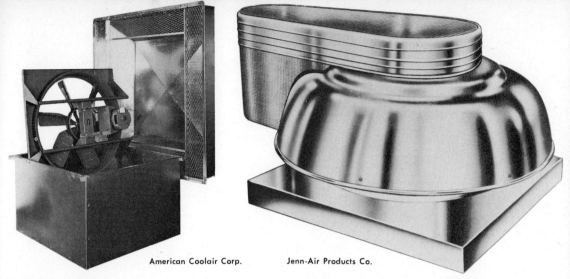

American Coolair Corp.

Jenn-Air Products Co.

An industrial exhaust fan with hood lifted back; this model is roof-mounted for vertical discharge of air.

A centrifugal type roof exhauster commonly used in schools, churches, hospitals, and office buildings.

these places must provide more than the normal number of cubic feet of fresh air per person, it is usually done by motor-driven devices. Various kinds of big fans or "blowers" do the job well. Suction fans, for example, suck stale air out of a factory with their huge blades; new air replaces the old through incoming ventilation tubes known as *ducts*.

Air Conditioning

AIR CONDITIONING is a special kind of ventilation. The difference is that an air-conditioning system does not have to depend on outside conditions in the atmosphere. It creates its own "climate" inside rooms, offices, auditoriums, stores, trains, even in automobiles and airplanes. The purpose of air conditioning is to make enclosed spaces more comfortable for human beings.

An air-conditioning unit not only "cools" the air, it regulates the humidity by taking some of the moisture out of the air it delivers to a room, controls the flow of air around a room, and removes unwanted dust, smoke, and odors.

An air conditioner takes the warm air from a room and passes it

37

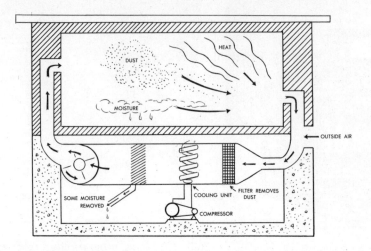

DUST

MOISTURE

HEAT

OUTSIDE AIR

SOME MOISTURE REMOVED

COOLING UNIT

FILTER REMOVES DUST

COMPRESSOR

One type of air-conditioning system used in homes today. This system not only cools air in summer, but filters out impurities, removes moisture, and draws new supplies of air from outside.

across cooling coils, much like those inside a refrigerator. Cooler and drier air is then passed back into the room and the temperature is thus reduced.

How Water Vapor Leaves the Air

WATER VAPOR gets into the troposphere mostly by evaporation. It leaves the air by *condensation* — the process by which water vapor changes into liquid water or ice crystals again.

Condensation *can only happen* when the water vapor is *cooled* to a certain limit called the *dew point*. The dew point is the temperature at which the saturation of air takes place. That temperature can be almost any temperature, depending on the absolute humidity. The more water vapor in the air, the higher the dew point; the less water vapor, the lower the dew point.

In general, there are four ways in which water vapor can cool to the dew point and condense: it mixes with colder air; it radiates its heat away into surrounding air; it hits cold surfaces such as icebergs, snow, or ground; it expands and cools when swept up by air currents.

When water vapor hits a cold surface near the ground, such as a housetop, a street, a blade of grass, or an automobile, it can condense in two forms. If the temperature is above freezing, it condenses as *dew*. If the temperature is below freezing, water vapor can condense directly out of the air, without passing through the liquid stage, as *frost*.

Fog and How It Forms

FOG is a kind of cloud resting right on or near the ground. But it is *not* made by water vapor touching cool ground surfaces and condensing out as dew or frost. Fog forms right in the air, but close to the ground.

When a layer of air that is anywhere from a few feet to a few hundred feet above the earth cools off to or below the dew point, the water vapor condenses to form *fog*. Fog is really millions and millions of tiny water droplets that gather together on the dust particles that are always present in the air. Each *droplet* is only about one ten-thousandth of an

Fog in this valley appears as a large lake of clouds when seen from above on a mountain slope. Note cirrostratus clouds high overhead.

U.S. Weather Bureau

inch in diameter, so that you would need to put together many, many thousands of them before you could even begin to see one *drop* of water. If the temperature is very cold, fog can be formed of tiny *ice crystals* instead of water droplets.

Fog is really water in the air; it is no longer water *vapor*. Why then doesn't it drop right to the ground, since water is heavier than air? Actually, the water droplets forming the fog *are* falling earthward every minute, but they are so light and falling so slowly that the tiniest breeze can keep them suspended or "hovering" above the ground.

Clouds and How They Form

SUPPOSE you are looking up at a very high mountain lost in a cloud. It may be a cloud to you, but to a person on the mountaintop it would be fog. Clouds, like fogs, are made of the countless numbers of tiny water droplets or ice crystals that have condensed out of the air, and that are clinging to their dust-particle "cores."

Also like fogs, clouds are produced when the air of the lower troposphere is cooled off to the dew point. But because clouds are really "high-flying" fogs, they are generally formed through the action of rising air.

Sometimes air rises when thicker, heavier air shoves up under it like a wedge. Sometimes winds or air currents push air up the sides of mountains. Often currents of air rise on hot, humid days.

The higher air rises, the more it expands because there is less pressure on it from the heavier, lower air. And the more it rises and expands, the faster it cools off due to lower temperatures. Cool air, however, cannot hold onto its water vapor as well as warm air. Its load of water becomes too great; saturation (capacity) is reached. That is the point when water droplets or ice crystals condense on the dust particles in the air. That is when a cloud is born.

How Clouds Are Named

IN THE YEAR 1896, the International Meteorological Committee met to classify the names of clouds. Before that time, so many different names had been used to describe clouds that weathermen in various countries did not understand each others' systems.

This Committee finally divided the different shapes of clouds into ten classes. Here they are, according to height:

cirrus cirrocumulus cirrostratus	20,000 ft. and higher	stratocumulus **stratus** nimbostratus	surface to 6,500 ft.
altocumulus altostratus	6,500 ft. to 20,000 ft.	**cumulus** cumulonimbus	1,600 ft. to cirrus level

You will see that the three clouds with the shortest names are printed in **dark letters.** These three represent the basic cloud shapes, and the other seven are different combinations of the basic three. (The end-papers of this book show photos of the 10 cloud types.)

Cirrus means "curly." Cirrus clouds, as their name indicates, are curly, white, and feathery. They are the highest of the clouds, ranging from about five to ten miles above the earth. So high are they, that their vapor is nearly always frozen into ice crystals. Sometimes high, curly cirrus clouds are called "mares' tails."

The next basic cloud shape is called *stratus,* meaning "spread out." Stratus clouds float in sheets or layers near the earth's surface. Sometimes "high fogs" are spoken of as stratus clouds.

Cumulus, the third type of cloud, means "heaped up." Cumulus clouds are like huge, puffy, heaped-up cotton balls. They are formed by air currents that move up from the earth. Usually, "pure" cumulus

U.S. Weather Bureau

**TWO UNUSUAL
CLOUD TYPES**
*(see endpapers for
10 basic types)*

Thunder ahead! These are cumulonimbus clouds called "anvil tops." They indicate great air disturbance (turbulence) and bring thunderstorms with them.

These stratocumulus clouds with hanging bulges are produced by strongly conflicting air masses. Often they indicate a tornado is coming.

U.S. Weather Bureau

clouds ride low above the earth in fair weather, and are thought by many to be the most beautiful of clouds. John Ruskin, the English poet, once called them "cloud chariots."

Usually, however, the clouds that you see in the sky are not "pure" examples of the three basic shapes, but combinations of them. *Cirrocumulus* clouds, for example, would have the characteristics of both cirrus and cumulus clouds. They would be heaped up, very high, and would be composed of ice crystals. *Cirrostratus* clouds would also be very high, layerlike clouds.

Nimbus means "raincloud" and *alto* means "high." When either of these two words are attached to the three basic types, they take on these meanings. For example, *cumulonimbus* clouds would be low-lying, heaped-up clouds, dark with rain. And *altocumulus* clouds would be high-flying, cumulus-type.   Alto- and cirrocumulus often give the effect of what weathermen call a "mackerel sky," because they resemble the patterns on a mackerel's back.

Precipitation — Rain, Snow, Sleet, Hail

THE OLD SAYING, "What goes up, must come down," is also true of water vapor that condenses out of the air into clouds. This happens by *precipitation,* which means "falling downward." Moisture *precipitates* — falls — from clouds to the earth below.

Scientists, even today, are not exactly sure when and how clouds precipitate their moisture. In very thick clouds, it may be that the small water droplets or ice crystals grow larger by more condensation or by joining with other droplets or crystals. Or, they may become larger in other ways. However this happens, when the droplets or ice crystals, or both, become too heavy to be supported by the air currents swirling about them, they fall earthward.

This moisture, of course, evaporates as it falls, but not completely

43

or it would never reach the ground. This is why people on mountain tops sometimes experience rain, while those at sea level in the same vicinity do not. The drops have evaporated somewhere between the top of the mountain and sea level.

Precipitation can take many different forms. The mildest of these is called *drizzle*. Drizzle is not-quite-rain. It is made up of very fine water droplets that are falling slowly and close together. They are seldom larger than one-fiftieth of an inch in diameter. When water droplets reach a diameter of about one-tenth of an inch, they are "droplets" no longer. They are then full-fledged *raindrops,* that fall to the earth much farther apart than droplets of drizzle.

Snow is a familiar kind of precipitation. You may have heard some-one say that snow is "frozen rain." This is not true. Snow is made of water vapor particles that have been changed right into crystals without having first passed into liquid form. They can only form when the dew point is below freezing. When more water vapor freezes around these crystals, they build up in size to form flat, six-sided *snowflakes.*

When snowflakes fall into warm air, they melt together and reach the ground as heavy, wet, "good-packing" snow. Of course, if the flakes melt completely, they fall as plain raindrops.

Snowflakes are still a mystery to scientists. The next time it snows,

Photographs of snow crystals as they appear under a microscope.

American Museum of Natural History

U.S. Weather Bureau

Boys holding hailstones as big as baseballs.

U.S. Weather Bureau

One of the huge hailstones that fell on Oklahoma in the *summer* of 1940!

catch a few on some dark paper and look at them under a magnifying glass. Why are they nearly always six-sided and six-pointed? Why are they always flat, instead of round like raindrops? One scientist spent over fifty years examining snowflakes and never found two alike.

The precipitation called *sleet,* however, *is* frozen rain. Sometimes in winter, when raindrops fall through freezing layers of air close to the ground, they freeze into little pellets of ice. *Ice storms,* on the other hand, occur only when rain freezes on direct contact with the ground, or things on the ground. Go and look at a forest just after an ice storm, and you will see one of the most beautiful sights nature has to offer.

Hailstones are like sleet particles, but much more complicated. They are onionlike layers of alternating clear ice and snow. When water vapor from a cloud condenses as water droplets, the droplets are sometimes swept upward where snow crystals are. This gives them a wrapping of snowflakes. Becoming heavier, they fall down again into freezing cloud levels and get a coating of raindrops. If they swirl upward again, that rain freezes on them and they get another shell of snowflakes. This can happen over and over again. Hailstones have been found with as many as twenty-five layers of snow and ice. They can be as small as a pea, or as large as a baseball.

45

U.S. Air Force Photo

"Contrails" (condensation trails). This remarkable photo shows Air Force bombers producing artificial cirrus clouds called "contrails" by means of their exhausts and propellers.

Costly winter wonderland created by an ice storm. Damage to power lines is being inspected after a storm near Albany, N.Y.

U.S. Weather Bureau

Hailstorms are produced by summer thunderstorms. They are great troublemakers, especially to farmers, and just one of them can cause millions of dollars' worth of damage. In some areas of our country, no farmer would think of being without hail insurance.

The Many Names of Moving Air

STEPHEN FOSTER, the American composer, once wrote a song about a girl named Jeanie. Jeanie had hair that "moved like a zephyr on the soft summer air." A *zephyr* is just one word for air that moves very gently and softly.

There are many words for moving air because air is moving practically all the time. Seldom does a region of air stand completely still; when one does, it is called a *calm*.

On a hot summer day we are glad to feel a *breeze* or a light *wind*. We are not so glad when the wind increases to a *gale*. Certainly no one is very happy when a gale develops into a raging snow-filled *blizzard,* a howling, twisting *tornado,* or a savage, destructive *hurricane, typhoon,* or *cyclone*.

There seem to be as many names for moving air as there are countries in the world. France has its dry, cold *mistral*. The northwestern area of the United States has its warm, moist *chinook*. Italy has its hot, dust-laden *sirocco* from the Libyan desert. India has its *monsoons;* Spain its *solano;* Russia its *buran;* Egypt its *khamsin;* and South America its *pampero* and *williwaws*.

But in general moving air is known simply as *wind,* and the most familiar winds are named for *the direction from which they come.* Thus, a *north wind* does not blow from the south to north, but *from the north.* Likewise, a *south wind* brings us warm air from the south. And a *sea breeze* comes from the sea, bringing the saltiness we so often smell at the seashore. What causes wind, anyway? How do winds start? Where do they blow to?

How the World's Wind System Works

SUPPOSE that the earth is standing quite still in space, neither rotating on its axis nor orbiting around the sun. Suppose also that the surface of the earth is one vast ocean. Under these conditions, how would the air of the atmosphere move?

First, the air at the equator — being nearest the sun and receiving the sun's direct rays — would become warm and rise. Underneath this rising air, in the lower atmosphere at the equator, a region of low pressure — due to high temperature — would be created. Farther north and south, however, the low-lying air would be cooler and heavier. These cool areas would be ones of high pressure due to the lower temperature. With the rising of the warm air at the equator, the highest pressure of the colder, heavier air would force that air toward the equator. In turn, it too would become warmed by the sun and rise. Then more of the cooler air underneath would be forced equatorward. *Air moves from regions of higher air pressure to regions of lower air pressure.*

Meanwhile, what is happening to the air far above the equator? There, too, a high pressure area is being created, because the rising air is adding its weight to the air that is already there.

What about the higher regions to the north and south of the equator? There the pressure is not so high. The sun's rays are striking the surface of the water at more of an angle; less air rises because less is heated. Naturally, the air at the poles would be heated least of all; less of it would rise and the pressure aloft would be quite low.

Thus, high in the atmosphere, there would be a sort of *pressure slope* from the equator to the poles. The upper air at the equator, always

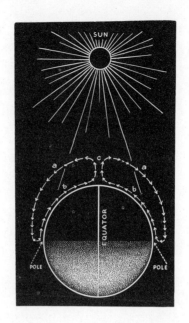

How the air of the atmosphere would move if the earth stood still in space and its surface were entirely ocean. At upper altitudes (a), flow would be toward poles. At lower levels (b), it would be toward the equator, and upward at or near the equator (c).

getting new supplies of rising air, would begin "falling" down toward the poles. In turn, lower in the atmosphere, there would be a drift of air toward the equator. Why? Because the air is following the path of least resistance — it is traveling toward the low pressure areas created by the warm, rising air at the equator.

Thus, on either side of the equator there would be a constant circulation of air toward the two poles, one clockwise and the other counterclockwise.

But remember, we have been talking about an earth that is one vast ocean, that is not rotating, that is standing still in space. While there *is* a general air-drift toward the poles aloft and another toward the equator lower down in the atmosphere, the real movement of air over the earth is affected by a number of other things.

Let's start our earth spinning again, add the land areas we call continents, and see what happens to moving air.

49

Sea and Land Breezes

ONE of the reasons why moving air does not circulate perfectly as described above is that the mixture of land and sea areas makes it impossible. Mainly, it is the differences in temperature between the two that cause varying air circulation.

Water does not warm up as fast as land, nor does it cool off as quickly. Water reflects more of the sun's rays than it soaks up; also, constant evaporation on the surface has a cooling effect. On the other hand, water does not radiate its heat away easily; what heat it has, it keeps for long periods.

Land, however, soaks up the sun's rays easily, without reflecting many of them. Thus, land is quickly warmed. Yet, it is quickly cooled, too, for the sun's rays do not penetrate very far beneath the surface. This makes land cool off rapidly at night.

Because land and sea areas vary sharply in temperature, there are *sea* and *land breezes*. In the daytime, a coastline warms up more quickly from the sun's rays than the water offshore does. Thus warm air rises from the land and is replaced by cooler sea air. Such a wind, blowing landward from the sea by day, is called a *sea breeze*.

How sea and land breezes blow.

SEA BREEZE (DAYTIME)

WARM AIR RISES OVER LAND

COOL SEA AIR FLOWS LANDWARD

LAND BREEZE (NIGHTTIME)

WARM SEA AIR RISES

COOL LAND AIR FLOWS SEAWARD

The opposite happens at night. The sea has kept its heat while the land has quickly cooled off. Warm air rising over the sea is replaced by cooler air from the land. Such a wind, blowing at night from the land toward the sea, is called a *land breeze*.

Monsoon Winds

SEA AND LAND "breezes" can also happen on a much larger scale. They can take place over whole continents and oceans — not by day and night, but *by season*. When, for example, the enormous land mass of Asia becomes heated in the summer, great quantities of warm air rise from it. The cooler, heavier air from the oceans to the south and east then flows landward. This makes a seasonal wind called a *summer monsoon. Monsoon* is an old Arabic word meaning "season."

In winter, the Asiatic continent loses its heat and grows colder than the seas. When the warmer air from the oceans rises, the cooler land air is forced seaward. This makes a wind called the *winter monsoon*. The best-known monsoon winds are those that flow over southeast Asia, India, and the Indian Ocean.

Moving air is also affected by things that get in its way on the earth itself — buildings, trees, mountains, and other obstructions. Winds tend to blow more steadily over smooth places such as oceans and plains than over rough places. Within a big city, for example, with its many buildings, winds are often broken up into tricky spurts called *gusts* and little whirlpools known as *eddies*.

How the Earth's Rotation Affects Moving Air

BECAUSE the earth spins on its axis, it acts like a giant turntable that is always sliding out from under the blanket of moving air above it. Be-

51

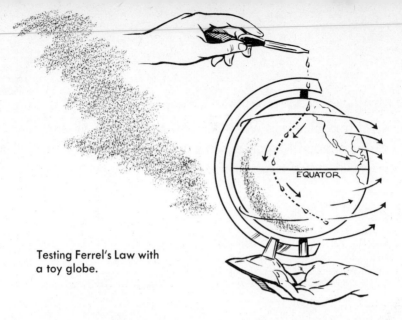

Testing Ferrel's Law with
a toy globe.

cause this is so, winds do not move exactly north and south, but are *deflected,* or turned aside.

This was first demonstrated in 1856 by an American scientist, William Ferrel. Ferrel's Law states: *because of the earth's rotation, winds in the northern hemisphere are deflected to the right; and winds of the southern hemisphere are deflected to the left.*

To understand Ferrel's Law, you must "put yourself in the picture" and face the right direction. Standing in the northern hemisphere and facing the equator, a wind — whatever its direction — would be turned to the right by the earth's rotation. Standing in the southern hemisphere and facing the equator, a wind — whatever its direction — would be turned to the left. The earth's rotation turns aside all winds in this way, with one exception — a wind blowing right along the equator would not be turned right or left.

You can prove Ferrel's Law by getting a toy globe of the earth and spinning it fast from west to east. At the north pole, start some colored water rolling in a stream south toward the equator with a medicine dropper. In the northern hemisphere, the stream turns to the right (pretending you are on the globe, too, looking toward the equator). But when the stream crosses the equator, it will start turning to the left.

52

The World's Wind Belts

IF IT were not for changing sea and land temperatures, the earth's rotation, and other things affecting moving air, winds would probably blow directly from high pressure areas to low pressure areas as shown in the "ideal" diagram on page 49.

But as we have seen, they do not. There are, however, certain belts of winds over the earth's surface that blow more or less steadily for months at a time.

The doldrums. This is a belt of low pressure along the equator where light winds vary with calms. It is caused by the constant rising of warm air heated by the sun's direct rays. The name "doldrums" goes back to the days of sailing ships (coming probably from the English word "dull") for in this belt vessels would lie becalmed for weeks. Some ships' captains even spoke of winds there that "blew up the masts"!

Actual distribution of wind belts over the earth's surface.

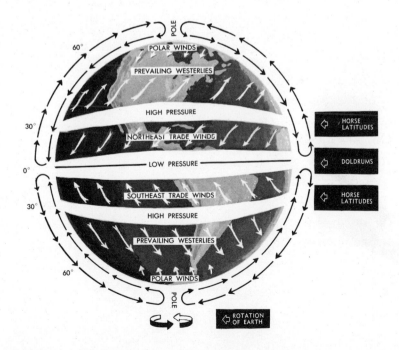

The trades and anti-trades. North and south of the doldrums in each hemisphere are the trade winds. The trades represent the moving air, close to the earth, that is always blowing toward the low pressure area of the equator. They blow steadier in one direction than any other winds. The name "trade" means "course" or "path," for these winds keep on pretty much of a straight course.

According to Ferrel's Law, the trades in the northern hemisphere are turned to the right and blow from the northeast to the southwest. Thus they are known as the "northeast trades." In the southern hemisphere, the trades are turned to the left and blow from the southeast to the northwest. They are therefore known as the "southeast trades."

As the word "anti" suggests, the anti-trades blow in the opposite direction from the trades. They represent the moving air much farther up in the troposphere than the low-lying trades. These are the winds that "fall down" the *pressure slope* from the equator to the poles. The anti-trades blow from the southwest in the northern hemisphere, and from the northwest in the southern hemisphere.

The horse latitudes. These are belts of alternating winds and calms beyond the trades centered about latitude 30° north and 30° south. They are twin belts of high pressure made by the air that has risen in the doldrums and is now descending. As in the doldrums the movement of the air is largely vertical, but this time *downward*. Thus, surface winds here are weak, and often absent.

Just how the horse latitudes got their unusual name is not certain. One story is that in colonial days, ships carrying horses to the West Indies were sometimes becalmed so long that the horses' food and water gave out and the animals had to be thrown overboard.

The prevailing westerlies. These are winds that tend to blow toward the north and south poles, but are turned aside by the earth's rotation. In the northern hemisphere, they become southwest winds, often called "southwesterlies." In the southern hemisphere, they blow from the north and west and are sometimes called "northwesterlies." "Prevailing" means that these winds blow from one direction more than from any other, and are stronger over smooth ocean surfaces than over land. Since there is more ocean area in the southern hemisphere than in the northern, the westerlies are very strong in that area. So strong are they in the latitudes between 40° and 50° south that they are often called the "roaring forties."

The polar winds. Finally, there are the belts of violent winds at the north and south poles. These generally blow from the very cold polar regions toward the equator again. They, too, are turned aside by the earth's rotation, causing them to become northeast winds in the northern hemisphere, and southeast winds in the southern. For this reason, they are sometimes known as the "polar easterlies."

What Are Jet Streams?

DURING World War II, American bombers, flying at great heights over Japan, ran into violent uncharted winds moving well over 200 miles an hour. Sometimes they were so strong that the crews had to turn back from their missions.

What the American pilots had run into was a *jet stream* — one of the fastest so far known — that sometimes races over Japan at 400 miles an hour!

Jet streams are found high in the upper troposphere, usually at altitudes from 30,000 to 50,000 feet. They are narrow, swift rivers of air that flow from west to east in a curving path around the earth. Jet streams are so-called because they are really swift *jets* of air that move faster than the air at either side, above, or below them. If the core of a jet stream is moving, say, at 250 miles an hour, the air several miles away might only be moving at half that speed.

Gliders like these are used to study jet-stream flow. Wispy cirrus clouds like the one below often indicate jet streams are present.

Just what causes jet streams is still unknown, but many times long, wispy cirrus clouds called *streamers* show that one is present. To find out more about these swift bands of air, scientists track them with radar or radio-transmitting devices attached to high-flying balloons. Already they know that the strongest occur in winter, and on the eastern sides of continents, such as the one over Japan.

Jet streams are also important in predicting the weather. Many weathermen are sure that they help *make* weather conditions below them because of their great speed and force. By tracking the path of a jet stream, weathermen can sometimes tell where it will go next and what kind of weather it will bring.

Air Pollution and the "Smog Barrier"

PRETEND for a minute that you live in an industrial town, perhaps in the Los Angeles Basin, or in the Upper Ohio River Valley. On certain days, the air is smokier or hazier than usual. Your eyes smart and sting; tears flow. Your throat feels scratchy. Your voice rasps. Breathing is difficult. Above you hovers grayish, foggy-looking air. Cars inch along with headlights on, although it is "daylight." The sun is only a faint, glowing ball overhead. Buildings are hard to make out. Things made of rubber crack; plants wilt and die.

What you are experiencing is a type of air pollution called "smog" — a mixture of *smoke* and *fog*. Sometimes it may be called "smaze" — a mixture of *smoke* and h*aze*. The air that we breathe can become *polluted* — made impure and unclean — in many ways. Dust storms throw up tiny particles of dirt that do not belong in the air. Forest fires fling up large quantities of smoke and gas. Animal and plant remains, plus the pollen from living plants, are also whipped into the air by winds.

But it is man himself who has done much to pollute his own air. It began when his first fires poured forth smoke. As human industry has developed, the rate at which man has polluted the air has increased tremendously. Belching smokestacks send incredible numbers of particles and gases skyward each year. Fumes from the exhaust pipes of millions of trucks and automobiles throw up countless more unwanted particles daily.

Weather Bureau officials first used the term "smog" in 1926; since then, it has become the word most often used to describe polluted air conditions in industrial areas.

Smog is smoke *plus* fog. But it is the smoke that helps make ordinary fog much worse. Industrial smoke released into the surrounding air consists of small particles, such as carbon soot and fly-ash. These particles help more fog to form, for they provide more cores on which water vapor in the air can collect. When this "smoke-fog" blankets an area, it holds up these unwanted particles and keeps them from escaping into the upper air.

Smog is most apt to occur in communities where a *temperature inversion* develops. This is an "upside-down" condition of the atmosphere. Often it happens on calm, clear nights when the ground rapidly cools.

Smog over Los Angeles, California. Identical views of the city on different days show how attacks vary in intensity.

The surface air is thus cooler than the air higher up. Being denser and heavier, it hugs the ground, trapping the polluted material in it.

The well known smogs of the Los Angeles area are caused by frequent temperature inversions. There, as early as 1542, Spanish explorers reported a smog attack caused by the smoke from Indian fires! Great air masses from the Pacific Ocean warm up as they descend on the Los Angeles Basin. This results in a warm layer of air, sometimes 2000 feet thick, overlying the cooler air beneath. The surrounding mountains prevent the underlying cool air from escaping and the weak winds cannot replace the old air with new. Underneath, of course, the eye-

How a temperature inversion layer creates smog conditions. This diagram was published in a Los Angeles area newspaper.

Los Angeles County Air Pollution Control District

WHY WE HAVE SMOG

1. AIR MASS FROM PACIFIC IS HEATED IN DESCENT TOWARD LOS ANGELES BASIN

2. CREATES UPSIDE-DOWN CLIMATE... WARM AIR ABOVE AND OCEAN-COOLED AIR BELOW

3. THIS IS THE TEMPERATURE INVERSION LAYER THAT HOLDS SMOG IN OUR BASIN

4. AND WINDS ARE TOO WEAK TO MOVE SMOG OUT OF BASIN

LOS ANGELES BASIN

smarting, throat-irritating smog in the Los Angeles Basin can be held in for days.

Sometimes when poisonous gases are also released under smoggy conditions in industrial areas, air pollution can result in death. In 1948, a famous smog in Donora, Pennsylvania, lasted from October 27 to 31. It spread over an area some eight miles wide, causing the deaths of 20 persons and serious illness to 5000! So bad was this smog that the citizens of Donora complained they could not "see their hands in front of their faces." Investigations later showed that deadly sulfur dioxide gas had combined with smog to produce suffocation in the victims.

Whenever smog hangs over an area, one thing is sure: the inhabitants of that area must either leave or breathe the polluted air. What can man do to clean up his dirty air?

Weapons to Fight Air Pollution

MANY measures have been developed to clean up polluted air in industrial districts. "Settling chambers" have been attached to chimneys and smokestacks to trap smoke particles that settle by gravity when mixed

Steel mills in Donora, Pennsylvania.

158

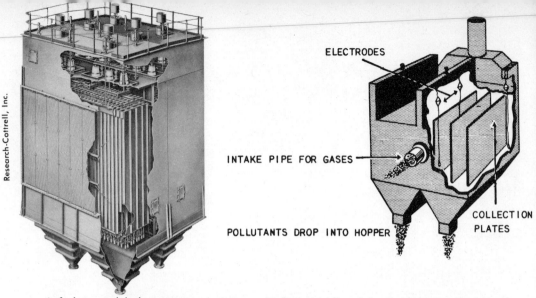

ELECTRODES

INTAKE PIPE FOR GASES

POLLUTANTS DROP INTO HOPPER

COLLECTION PLATES

Left: late model electrostatic precipitator. Right: principle of the precipitator. Device collects solid particles from fume-laden gases passing between electrodes. Electrodes charge the particles and attract them as a magnet does iron filings.

with certain gases. "Cyclone chambers" have also proved effective; in these, particles are caught up by whirling air and trapped in filtering devices. "Automatic stokers" used in furnaces that burn soft coal have reduced air pollution; so has the use of smokeless fuels like anthracite. Certain harmful gases are successfully removed from industrial smoke by passing them through a water spray device known as a "scrubber."

But it is a device called an *electrostatic precipitator* (shown above) that has probably been most effective in removing the smallest, most numerous particles from industrial smoke. An American chemist, Frederick G. Cottrell, developed it early in this century.

Aside from industrial smoke, bluish hazes caused by certain gases also hover over many large communities. The Dutch-American biologist, J. Haagen-Smit, was the first man to prove that this haze is made by gasoline vapors from motor vehicle exhaust pipes, and that it is one of the major sources of air pollution in Los Angeles County. When Dr. Haagen-Smit combined these vapors with ozone, he reproduced a typical Los Angeles smog, complete with haze.

Pittsburgh Is the "Smokeless City" Now

PITTSBURGH, Pennsylvania, was once known as the "smoky city." For decades dense columns of air-polluting smoke had belched forth into the air from steel furnaces and other industrial plants. But in 1947, severe anti-smoke laws went into effect in Pittsburgh.

Determined to clean up their city's polluted air, authorities urged plant and factory owners to take up new control measures. One by one, the factory owners had to do this. They installed smoke-control devices such as scrubbers and electrostatic precipitators. In addition, the use of soft coal for cooking and heating was forbidden.

In a short time, conditions improved amazingly. The air was purer and less hazy. Throats and eyes were no longer irritated. Pittsburgh today is no longer the "smoky city."

Like Pittsburgh, other cities and communities are also taking steps to get rid of their air pollution problems. Like the people of Pittsburgh, they want clean, fresh air to breathe — *air for today and tomorrow*.

"Raob" (radar-observer) balloon being sent to upper atmosphere to check temperatures, dew points, humidity, and wind velocities over atomic test site at Indian Springs Air Force Base, Nevada. Note "mares' tails" (cirrus clouds) floating high above. U.S. Air Force Photo

Simple Air Experiments You Can Do

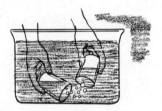

Prove that air is real and takes up space by "pouring" it underwater. Get a large pan and fill it with about eight inches of water. Next get two tall drinking glasses. Tip one sideways so that it fills with water. Force the second one straight down into the water (water can't get in because something else is already there — air). Hold the two glasses as shown in the picture and "pour" the air from the glass-full of air upward into the glass of water. Listen to the bubbling and gurgling as the air goes from one glass to another.

Understand relative humidity better by experimenting with a sponge, a pan, and a jar. Fill the pan with water, soak the sponge in the water until it holds all that it can hold, then empty the pan. Pretend the sponge is a block of air; it is now "saturated" because it is holding 100 per cent of its capacity of water. Now squeeze all the water out of the sponge into the jar where it can be measured with a ruler. Pour half of this water back into the empty pan. Soak the sponge again in the water the pan now holds. The sponge (block of air) now holds half the water it did before — it represents 50 per cent relative humidity.

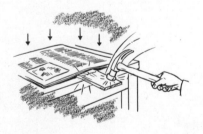

Prove how strong air pressure can be. Locate a wooden slat from an old crate about four feet long. Lay it on a table and let three to four inches of it extend off the table. Then lay some double sheets of newspaper over the part of the slat on the table, as shown. Get a hammer and sharply hit the part of the slat that extends over the table edge. The slat will probably break because the air is pressing down so hard on the paper.

Try the "index card" experiment to show the lowering of atmospheric pressure. Bend the card as shown in the picture and put it on the edge of a table. Ask a friend to upset the card by blowing *under* it. Your friend will find that it can't be done. By blowing under the card a low pressure area is created and the weight of normal air pressure on top of the card will keep it firmly in place.

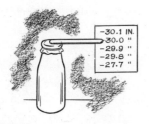

Make a simple homemade aneroid barometer with a milk bottle, as shown in the picture. Get some sheet rubber (a balloon will do) and stretch it tightly over the top of the bottle. Keep the sheet in place with rubber bands. Make a pointer out of a thin wooden splint and glue it to the top of the rubber sheet. Make a scale and point the pointer toward it so that you can read the changes in atmospheric pressure.

Prove that warm air rises and expands. Get a soda bottle, a balloon, and a pan. After squeezing all the air out of the balloon, fit the mouth of the balloon over the top of the soda bottle. Fill the pan with cool water and put the bottle in it. (So far nothing has happened, has it?) Next, place the pan over a gas range and heat the water in the pan. Soon the air inside the bottle will warm up. Then it will slowly rise, expand, and blow up the balloon.

Try the "ping-pong ball low-pressure" experiment. You will need two ping-pong balls, two pieces of string, a rod, and some plastic cement. Put a drop of cement on each of the ping-pong balls and attach the two strings. Hang the two balls side by side on the rod about two inches apart. Try blowing between the two balls to separate them. Instead, they come closer together! You have created a low pressure area between them by blowing the jet of air. The higher pressure of the air on the outsides of the balls forces them together.

Prove that air pressure pushes on things in all directions. Fill a milk bottle with water and cover it with a piece of cardboard. Holding the cardboard in place with your thumb, turn the bottle upside down. Remove your thumb carefully and the water will stay in the bottle! Why? Because the air pressure outside is greater than the weight of the water pressing downward inside the bottle. It holds up the water in the bottle.

Make a warm-air-current detector. Draw a spiral on some heavy paper or light cardboard, then cut it out with a pair of scissors. Make a hole in the center of the spiral and put a length of thread through it. Knot the thread so it will hold up the spiral. Test for warm air currents around your home by holding the detector as still as possible over a radiator, an electric light bulb, or other hot places. The spiral will rotate due to the upward-moving warm air.

Prove that air can be compressed by actually compressing some. Locate a bottle and a cork that fits it very tightly. Fill the bottle with water, but leave space enough for one small bubble. Put the cork into the bottle and start pressing on it. The harder you press, the smaller the bubble gets because the air molecules are jammed closer together — compressed. To make the bubble get bigger again, draw the cork back out slowly.

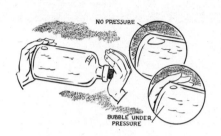

Prove that when air is warmed it expands, rises, and weighs less than the surrounding cooler air. You will need a thin dowel stick about three feet long, two small shopping bags the same size, and a candle. Scotch-tape the bags to either end of the stick upside-down, as shown. Tie a string to the middle of the stick and suspend it on something. Adjust the stick carefully so that the bags are balanced and level. Hold the lighted candle under one of the bags, keeping it far enough away so the bag will not catch fire. As the air inside the bag is heated, it becomes lighter and rises — and so does the bag.

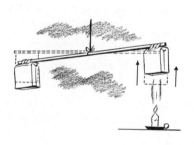

Prove that there is about one-fifth of a part of oxygen in the air by actually taking that much out of a sample of air. All you need is a very tall glass, a bowl of water and a small bit of birthday candle. Mount the candle on a small wooden or cork float, light it, and place it on top of the water in the bowl. Now hold the glass over the candle, with the mouth of the glass pushed down into the water. In a little while, the candle will go out because the flame has used up all the oxygen in the air. Meanwhile, the water has risen about a fifth of the way up into the glass to replace the lost oxygen.

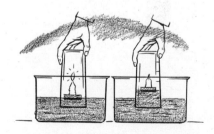

Index

Standard Oil Co. (N.J.)

American Museum of Natur

Above: Cirrostratus
Left: Stratocumulus
Below left: Altocumulus ("mackerel sky")
Below: Nimbostratus

U.S. Weather Bureau

American Museum of Natur

Left: Cumulonimbus

U.S. Navy Photo

U.S. Air Force Photo

Above: Altostratus over stratocumulus
Right: Stratus
Below: Cirrus ("mares' tails")

American Museum of Natural History

U.S. Weather Bureau

American Museum of Natural History

Below right: Cirrocumulus
Below: Cumulus

Florida State News Bureau

FIRST BOOKS

classified by subject

Some titles are listed in more than one category

The ARTS

Architecture	Gardening	Poetry
Ballet	How to Fix It	Puppets
Bells	Jazz	Rhythms
Color	Music	Stage Costume and
Drawing	Paintings	Make-Up
	Photography	

COMMUNICATIONS

Atlas	Letter Writing	Public Libraries
Codes and Ciphers	Maps and Globes	Teaching Machines
Language & How To	Measurement	Television
Use It	Printing	Words

SCIENCE

Air	Electricity	Roads
Airplanes	Food	Science Experiments
Antarctic	Glaciers	Sea Shells
Archaeology	Glass	Snakes
Architecture	Human Senses	Sound
Astronomy	Light	Space Travel
Automobiles	Machines	Stone Age Man
Bees	Mammals	Stones
Bells	Maps and Globes	Submarines
Birds	Measurement	Television
Bridges	Microbes	Tools
Bugs	Mining	Trains
Caves	Ocean	Trees
Color	Photography	Tropical Mammals
Conservation	Plants	Water
Cotton	Prehistoric Animals	Weather
Earth	Rhythms	Wild Flowers

SPORTS & HOBBIES

Baseball	Dogs	Photography
Basketball	Dolls	Physical Fitness
Boys' Cooking	Football	Sailing
Cartoons for Kids	Gardening	Stones
Cats	Horses	Surprising Facts
Chess	How to Fix It	Swimming
Christmas Joy	Jokes	
Codes and Ciphers	Magic	

SOCIAL STUDIES

United States

Atlas	Hawaii	Oregon Trail
American History	Holidays	Panama Canal
American Revolution	Indian Wars	Pioneers
California Gold Rush	Indians	Presidents
The China Clippers	National Monuments	Supreme Court
Civil War Land Battles	National Parks	United Nations
Civil War Naval Actions	Negroes	War of 1812
Congress	New England	Washington, D.C.
Constitution	New World Explorers	World War I
Early Settlers		World War II

The World About Us

Africa	Communist China	Mexico
Ancient Bible Lands	Congo	Netherlands
Ancient Egypt	England	New Zealand
Ancient Mesopotamia	Eskimos	Ocean
and Persia	Festivals	Pakistan
Ancient Greece	France	South America
Ancient Rome	Ghana	Soviet Union
Antarctic	India	United Nations
Archaeology	Israel	Vikings
Australia	Italy	West Germany
Barbarian Invaders	Japan	West Indies
Brazil	Kings	World War I
Canada	Medieval Man	World War II
	Mediterranean	

People and Products

Conservation	Firemen	Nurses
Cotton	Food	Supermarkets
Cowboys	Glass	Water

LITERATURE & LANGUAGE ARTS

Codes and Ciphers	Letter Writing	Norse Legends
Color	Legendary Beings	Poetry
Fairy Tales	Maps and Globes	Printing
Language & How To	Mythology	Teaching Machines
Use It	Mythical Beasts	Words

TRANSPORTATION

Airplanes	Maps and Globes	Space Travel
Automobiles	Panama Canal	Trains
Boats	Roads	Water
Bridges	Ships	